Hide and Seek

**Written by Tobia Rossi,
translated by Carlotta Brentan**

T0346832

methuen | drama

LONDON • NEW YORK • OXFORD • NEW DELHI • SYDNEY

METHUEN DRAMA
Bloomsbury Publishing Plc
50 Bedford Square, London, WC1B 3DP, UK
1385 Broadway, New York, NY 10018, USA
29 Earlsfort Terrace, Dublin 2, Ireland

BLOOMSBURY, METHUEN DRAMA and the Methuen
Drama logo are trademarks of Bloomsbury Publishing Plc

First published in Great Britain 2024

Nascondino © Tobia Rossi, 2019

Translation copyright © Carlotta Brentan, 2024

Tobia Rossi and Carlotta Brentan have asserted their right under the Copyright,
Designs and Patents Act, 1988, to be identified as authors of this work.

Cover image: Mariano Gobbi

Bloomsbury Publishing Plc does not have any control over, or responsibility
for, any third-party websites referred to or in this book. All internet addresses
given in this book were correct at the time of going to press. The author and
publisher regret any inconvenience caused if addresses have changed or sites
have ceased to exist, but can accept no responsibility for any such changes.

No rights in incidental music or songs contained in the work are hereby
granted and performance rights for any performance/presentation
whatsoever must be obtained from the respective copyright owners.

All rights whatsoever in this play are strictly reserved and application
for performance etc. should be made before rehearsals by professionals
and by amateurs to Permissions Department, Methuen Drama,
Bloomsbury Publishing Plc, 50 Bedford Square, London
WC1B 3DP Performance.Permissions@bloomsbury.com.
No performance may be given unless a licence has been obtained.

A catalogue record for this book is available from the British Library.

A catalog record for this book is available from the Library of Congress.

ISBN: PB: 978-1-3504-9702-3
ePDF: 978-1-3504-9703-0
eBook: 978-1-3504-9704-7

Series: Modern Plays

Typeset by Mark Heslington Ltd, Scarborough, North Yorkshire
Printed and bound in Great Britain

To find out more about our authors and books visit
www.bloomsbury.com and sign up for our newsletters.

ZAVA Productions in association with Lorenzo Mannelli and Park Theatre presents

Hide and Seek

Written by Tobia Rossi

Translated and directed by Carlotta Brentan

INTERNATIONAL JOURNEY OF THE PLAY

The play was originally written by Tobia Rossi in Italian with the title *Nascondino*. The play won the 2019 Mario Fratti Award at In Scena! Italian Theater Festival NY, presented by Kairos Italy Theater, KIT Italia and Casa Italiana Zerilli-Marimo' at NYU.

In May 2022 Kairos Italy Theater and The Tank produced the worldwide premiere of the English translation at The Tank NYC. Translated and directed by Carlotta Brentan.

Hide and Seek had its UK premiere in London at VAULT Festival in February 2023 produced by ZAVA Productions in co-production with Kairos Italy Theater.

WRITER'S NOTE

If in this day and age we are supposedly free to embrace our LGBTQ+ identities, why is it that we keep witnessing instances of homophobic violence? In Italy, where I'm from, laws to criminalise homophobia struggle to gain enough support. It's almost as if two different realities coexist in my country: an inclusive Italy where diversity is loudly embraced and celebrated, and a hidden Italy that is kept secret, yet is perhaps more deeply rooted. A country where sexual orientation and gender identity are still cause for profound embarrassment and exclusion, where being different is taboo and mob mentality shapes young minds and forges identities. *Hide and Seek* aims to be a dark fairy tale, a coming-of-age story that explores these contradictions and their most extreme and terrifying consequences.

WHY *Hide and Seek* NOW?

The play explores issues that are – sadly – still pressing today: homophobia, bullying, and how when young minds are exposed to such forces in their formative years, their world view is indelibly shaped by their toxicity in ways that can't be measured or controlled. *Hide and Seek* meaningfully presents these subjects through the youthful, naive, unexpectedly insightful gaze of two teenagers, who are desperate to find in each other the freedom of being themselves.

We hope our audience will join us on Gio and Mirko's compelling, dark, funny and truthfully presented journey of discovery – of their true identity, of their place in the world. We hope to stimulate reflection and spark conversation about how vulnerable young minds are to discriminatory and exclusionary voices in their environment, and how strongly these internalised messages of hate can take root.

Special thanks to: Il Circolo – Italian Cultural Association, The Sylvia Waddilove Foundation UK, Com.It.Es di Londra and BIS – British Italian Society, Gendered Intelligence, Laura Caparrotti and Lorenzo Mannelli and the many supporters from our crowdfunding campaign.

CAST

GIO | **LORIS SCARPA**

MIRKO | **NICO CETRULO**

Loris Scarpa | GIO

Loris graduated from the Actor Musicianship course at Rose Bruford College in 2021. Theatre credits include: *Once* (The London Palladium, Tokyu Orb, China Tour), *Rapunzel* (The Watermill Theatre), *Alice in Wonderland* (The Mercury Theatre), *Glory Ride* (The Charing Cross Theatre). Screen and voiceover credits include: *Sweetpea* (Sky Atlantic), *SAS: Rogue Heroes* (BBC), *Doctors* (BBC), *Pin Cushion* (BFI), *Company of Heroes* (Relic Entertainment).

Nico Cetrulo | MIRKO

Nico Cetrulo trained at Arts Educational, where productions included *Hamlet, Chaos and Confusions.* Work in theatre includes *The Merchant of Venice* and *Sapho & Phao* for the RSC and Zava Production's *Hide and Seek* for VAULT Festival. Short films include *How to Get Away with Murder.*

CREATIVE TEAM

WRITER | **TOBIA ROSSI**

TRANSLATOR AND DIRECTOR I **CARLOTTA BRENTAN**

MUSIC COMPOSER | **SIMONE MANFREDINI**

FIGHT DIRECTOR | **MICHAEL O'DONNELL**

SET DESIGNER I **CONSTANCE COMPAROT**

LIGHTING DESIGNER | **ALEX FOREY**

STYLIST | **ALESSANDRO MILZONI**

DRAMATURG AND ASSISTANT DIRECTOR | **GIADA PRESTINARI**

PRODUCTION STAGE MANAGER | **FAE HOCHGEMUTH**

PRODUCTION ASSISTANT | **ASTRID GALETTO**

CASTING | **LAURA SEABORN FOR HJB CASTING**

MARKETING I **LIAM MCLAUGHLIN**

CONTENT CREATOR I **MARIANO GOBBI**

PRODUCER AND GENERAL MANAGER | **ZAVA PRODUCTIONS**

ASSOCIATE PRODUCER | **LORENZO MANNELLI**

CO-PRODUCER | **KAIROS ITALY THEATER**

Tobia Rossi | Writer

Tobia is an Italian playwright and screenwriter working with the main Italian and Milanese theatres. His recent works include: *Il Principe dei sogni belli* (The prince of good dreams, 2020), *Garbo* (Grace, 2021) for *Abbecedario per il mondo nuovo* (Primer for the New World), Piccolo Theatre, Milan, 2021, and *I Signori dell'Universo* (The Lords of the Universe, 2021), presented at Centro Teatrale Bresciano. Tobia wrote the libretto for the opera *Troposfera*  (Troposphere), Venice Biennale Music, 2016, and the musicals *The Prince of Air* and *Miss I-Doll*, both recently showcased in London. Awards include: the honourable mention at the Hystrio Scritture per la

Scena_35 Award with *La cosa brutta* (The Ugly Thing, 2016), the Mario Fratti Award with *Nascondino* (Hide and Seek, 2019) and in 2023 the LGBTQ+ community and diversity in love International Award Carlo Annoni with *Piccola Bestia* (Little Beast). *Hide and Seek* has also become a novel with the title *Cosa siamo nel buio* (What We Are in the Dark), published by Mondadori Ragazzi. His first screenplay, co-written with Giada Bossi, is in development with Indiana Production. Tobia is also a story editor for TV and cinema and a creative writing teacher in Milan at Franco Parenti Theatre, Cinema Accademy Luchino Visconti and IED – Design European Institute.

Carlotta Brentan | Translator and Director

Carlotta is a New York-based bilingual theatre artist specializing in the development of brave, challenging new plays as a director, actor, producer and translator. Stage highlights: World premieres of Frank J. Avella's *Lured*, based on real events of anti-gay persecution in Russia (performed and co-directed, sold-out runs at Theater for The New City in NYC and OnStage! Festival in Rome), Avella's *Vatican Falls* about the Catholic Church sex abuse scandal (performed and co-directed, The Tank NYC), Paolo Bignami's *The Journey I Never Made* (performed and translated from Italian, Cherry Lane Theatre NYC), Erik Ehn's *Clover* (La MaMa Experimental Theater Club NYC). Carlotta has collaborated on the development of Tobia Rossi's *Hide and Seek* since 2019 as translator and director in both NYC and London, and is thrilled to continue this powerful play's journey at Park Theatre. Carlotta is also a film actor, prolific voiceover artist and award-winning audiobook narrator of over 200 novels. www.carlottabrentan.com

Simone Manfredini | Music Composer

Simone is a composer, pianist, orchestrator and conductor who has worked extensively in London and Europe for Disney Theatrical, Cameron Mackintosh LTD, Stage Entertainment, ATG and other world-class companies. His main credits as musical director include *The Lion King*, *Les Miserables*, *Mary Poppins*, *9 to 5*, *Mamma Mia!*, *Beauty and the Beast*, *Cats*, *Sister Act* and many others. Workshop includes: *The Prince of Air*, *Miss I-Doll, Sugar*, *Vanara*, *Confessions*, *Fat Friends*, *The Braille Legacy* and *The Little Prince*. Simone composed and arranged several pieces of music for theme parks, where he won the Parks Mania Award for best song and best show. He's the recipient of the Score the World 2023 award and his music is featured on the short film *Walking Fernando* with Javier Bardem. Simone is currently developing his own musical projects: *The Prince of Air*, *Miss I-Doll*, *In a State of Grace* and *Solstice*.

Michael O'Donnell | Fight Director

Michael started his artistic career in New York as performer in *Jerome Robbin's Broadway*, *Carousel* at Lincoln Centre, *Victor/Victoria* starring Julie Andrews, Sam Mendes' *Cabaret*, *Wonderful Town*, *The Pajama Game* with Harry Connick Jr. and *Spamalot*. Michael began his directing career staging the touring version of some of the Broadway productions where he performed, including *Cabaret* and *Spamalot*. He produced a full-length comedy film, *Moving Mike,* in Manhattan, 2009. He was Resident Director of Cameron Mackintosh's 25th anniversary tour of *Les Misérables*, 2011. He also produced and created exciting large-scale events from the ground up, most notably the annual Christmas party for mega agency McGarryBowen. Michael is currently the Supervising Resident Director of Disney's *The Lion King* in the West End and UK tour.

Constance Comparot | Set Designer

Constance is a French performance designer and theatre maker based in London. She trained in BA Theatre Design at Wimbledon College of Arts, UAL, and graduated in 2022. Her work as a set designer include *Fairytale on Church Street* (The Cockpit, 2023), *Homeless* (Camden Fringe 2023), *Persephone* (Edinburgh Fringe, 2023), *Mum* (Tramshed Theatre, 2023), *Poetry Brothel: I Spit Roses* (Century Club, 2023), *Kitty in the Lane* and *Paddy goes to Petra* (Brockley Jack, 2022/23), *Ascension* and *The One the River Didn't Keep* (Windsor Fringe festival, 2022 and 2023), *Last Night of Love*, *First Night of War* (Electrowerk, 2022), *Poetry Brothel: Death is My Lover* (Electrowerk, 2022), *Fear* (Middlesex University, 2021). As an assistant designer, she has worked for Opera Holland Park (*HMS Pinafore*, 2022) and the New Nordics Festival (2021). www.constancecomparot.com

Alex Forey | Lighting Designer

Alex is a lighting designer, associate, programmer and technician. He is a graduate of the Royal Academy of Dramatic Art. Lighting designer includes: *Polyeucte* (Theatre Royal Stratford East), *Libuše*, *Rhapsody 2019*, *From Here To Eternity* (Bloomsbury Theatre), *Babel* (Lyric Hammersmith), *Into The Woods*, *Exhibition* (Shaw Theatre), *Network*, *Killology*, *Mums*, *Till Death Do We Part*, *Honey Badger*, *Three Sisters*, *The Importance of Being Earnest*, *Electra*, *Yerma* and *The Tempest* (Wimbledon College of Art), *Message in a Clay River*, *A Sexual Odyssey*, *Written on the Body* (Cockpit Theatre), *Songs for a New World* (Drayton Arms Theatre), *The Piper of Hamelin* (Rose Theatre, Kingston), *Manifestos* (Bloomsbury Festival, RADA Studios), *Graduate Showcase 2019* (Italia Conti Academy), *Henry V*, *Hiroshima: Crucible of Light* (Samuel Pepys Theatre), *Grey Matter*, *Twelfth Night* (Edinburgh Fringe). Awards include: winner of the Vectorworks Design Scholarship 2020 (UK, Entertainment Category), UCL Arts Award for Best Design 2018 (joint with scenic design) for *Polyeucte* and UCL Arts Award for Best Design 2019 (lighting) for *Rhapsody 2019*. www.alexforey.com

For Park Theatre

Artistic Director
Jez Bond

Executive Director
Catherine McKinney

CREATIVE ENGAGEMENT

Community Engagement Manager
Carys Rose Thomas

DEVELOPMENT

Development Director
Tania Dunn

Development & Producing Coordinator
Ellen Harris

FINANCE

Finance Director
Elaine Lavelle

Finance Officer
Nicola Brown

Finance Assistant
Pinar Kurdik

GENERAL MANAGEMENT

General Manager
Tom Bailey

Deputy General Manager
David Hunter

Producer Programmer
Amelia Cherry

Administrator
Mariah Sayer

Access Coordinator
David Deacon

Duty Venue Managers
Leiran Gibson, Gareth Hackney, Zara Naeem, Laura Riseborough, Natasha Green, David Hunter, Shaun Joynson, Wayne Morris, Daisy Bates, Nick Raistrick

---

PARK PIZZA

Supervisors
Daisy Bates, Luke Brock

Bar Team
George Gehm, John Burman, Bradly Doko, Hugo Harrison, Alex Kristoffy, Vanessa Restivo, Bonnie Shapland-Hill, Julia Skinner, Maddie Stoneman, Maria Ziolkowska

---

SALES & MARKETING

Sales & Marketing Director
Dawn James

Head of Ticketing
Matthew Barker

Marketing Manager
Anna Charlesworth

Marketing Assistant
Conor Gormally

Senior Box Office Supervisor
Natasha Green

Box Office Supervisors
Jacquie Cassidy, Gareth Hackney, Kyanne Smith, Maddie Stoneman

Public Relations
Mobius Industries

TECHNICAL & BUILDING

Technical & Buildings Manager
Gianluca Zona

Deputy Technical & Buildings Manager
Teddy Nash

Venue Technician
Michael Bird

About Park Theatre

Park Theatre was founded by Artistic Director Jez Bond and Creative Director Emeritus Melli Marie. The building opened in May 2013 and, with 12 West End transfers, two National Theatre transfers and 14 national tours in ten years, quickly garnered a reputation as a key player in the London theatrical scene. Park Theatre has received six Olivier nominations, won numerous Off West End Offie Awards, and won *The Stage*'s Fringe Theatre of the Year and Accessible Theatre Award.

Park Theatre is an inviting and accessible venue, delivering work of exceptional calibre in the heart of Finsbury Park. We work with writers, directors and designers of the highest quality to present compelling, exciting and beautifully told stories across our two intimate spaces.

Our programme encompasses a broad range of work from classics to revivals with a healthy dose of new writing, producing in-house as well as working in partnership with emerging and established producers. We strive to play our part within the UK's theatre ecology by offering mentoring, support and opportunities to artists and producers within a professional theatre-making environment.

Our Creative Learning strategy seeks to widen the number and range of people who participate in theatre, and provides opportunities for those with little or no prior contact with the arts.

In everything we do we aim to be warm and inclusive; a safe, welcoming and wonderful space in which to work, create and visit.

★ ★ ★ ★ ★ "A five-star neighbourhood theatre" *Independent*

As a registered charity [number 1137223] with no public subsidy, we rely on the kind support of our donors and volunteers. To find out how you can get involved visit parktheatre.co.uk

Hide and Seek

Characters

Mirko *and* **Gio**, *teenagers*.

Place

A cave deep underground, somewhere in the middle of the woods, far away from town.

Darkness, mud, cold.

Time

Today. Autumn.

Scene One

Pitch-black darkness.

Mirko *– fancy backpack, designer sports jacket and a trendy haircut – is by the entrance of the cave. He catches a glimpse of* **Gio** *– wearing stained jeans and a dirty, worn-out jumper – who is hiding in the darkness next to a few indistinguishable objects, neatly piled up.*

Mirko *tries to shed some light with the torch on his phone.*

Mirko   Hey.

Gio   Hey.

Mirko   Are you okay?

Gio   I'm, okay, yeah.

Mirko   Is everything . . .

Gio   Yeah.

Mirko   . . . okay, I mean –

Gio   I'm okay.

A pause.

Mirko (*referring to his phone*)   Where can I put this?

Gio   What?

Mirko   So it makes more light.

Gio   On the ground.

Mirko   On the ground?

Gio   Facing up.

Mirko   It'll get dirty.

Gio   Oh.

Mirko   It'll get shit all over it.

Gio   Right.

Mirko   Like dirt and shit.

Gio   Use this.

Gio *grabs a magazine from his stack of objects and throws it to him.* **Mirko** *catches it.*

Mirko (*looking at the magazine*)   What's this?

Gio   So it doesn't get dirty.

Mirko *places the magazine on the ground and rests his phone on it facing up, so it emits a more diffuse light.* **Mirko** *and* **Gio** *study each other for a few moments.*

Mirko   I'll sit, I mean, can I sit?

Gio   Yeah, I can give you –

Mirko   It's fine.

Mirko *sits on his backpack.*

What about you?

Gio   What?

Mirko   Sit.

Gio *sits, keeping his distance.*

Mirko   That's not fair.

Gio   Why?

Mirko   I can't see you.

Gio   I can see you.

Mirko   Well sure, the light is in my face.

Gio *scoots closer.*

Mirko   There.

Gio   What?

Mirko   That's better.

Gio   Okay.

Mirko   Thanks. (*A pause, then referring to their surroundings.*)
What is this, a cavern, a . . .

Gio   A cave.

Mirko   How . . . How did you . . . end up here?

Gio   How did *you* end up here?

Mirko   I don't know, I – I saw there was a kind of, of, of
entrance. Half covered with dry leaves. And soil. At first I
thought it was a well . . . or one of those septic tanks.

Gio   Right.

Mirko   So I came down, to like, explore.

Gio   And what were you doing? In the middle of the woods?

Mirko   Nothing. Just like, hanging about. Shit, you must be
hungry. You want some Ringos?

Gio   Were you . . . were you looking for something?

Mirko *shrugs as he rifles through his backpack.*

Mirko   They say there's like, woodchucks and white hares
around here so I was just looking around. (*He pulls out a
packet of biscuits and sings the tune from the Ringo ad.*) *You're
always on top with Ringo!* They're so good, even though the ad
is fucking dumb, with Shade playing basketball with his
coach. You ever see it?

Gio   No.

Mirko   And it's obvious Shade doesn't give a fuck, he's just
doing it for the money. (*He eats a biscuit, talking with his mouth
full.*) You must be dying for a shower.

Gio   Do I stink?

Mirko   No.

Gio   I go to the toilet down here but I cover everything up with soil so you can't smell it.

Mirko   Relax, you don't –

Gio   You think I stink?

Mirko   No, like, even if you do, I can't smell it from here.

Gio   Oh.

Mirko   I have a very sensitive sense of smell so if you did, I would have noticed.

A pause.

Gio   Okay.

Mirko *goes on eating.* *He studies* **Gio**.

Mirko (*referring to his camera*)   Photos. That's why I'm out here. My dad lent me his Reflex camera. I've been watching this, like, photography course on TikTok. I want to practise with all kinds of stuff: portraits, landscapes, still life, wildlife. Today I wanted to do wildlife and they suggested I come here.

A pause.

Listen . . . is it true what they say about you?

Gio   That I only bathe with a full moon?

Mirko   No, like . . .

Gio   That I got crabs when I was in primary school and I still have them today?

Mirko   No, no, no . . .

Gio   That I kiss my dog on the mouth?

Mirko   I meant if it's true that you, like, *have some screws loose*.

Gio   What do you think?

Mirko   Oh, I don't know. Anyway, fuck that.

Gio   What do you mean?

Mirko   People can say what they want. I don't care. I think with my own head.

Gio   . . .

Mirko   You know why they say that stuff about you?

Gio   . . .

Mirko   'Cause they don't know you. And when people don't know someone, or something, they talk shit.

A pause.

Gio   Could I have a biscuit?

Mirko   Here.

Mirko *hands* **Gio** *a biscuit.*

Gio (*singing*)   *You're always on top with Ringo.*

Mirko *laughs.*

As he chews, **Gio** *stares intensely at* **Mirko***.*

Gio   Were you in the choir?

Mirko   I'm over it.

Gio   That's too bad. You were amazing when you played the lion.

Mirko   Fuck.

Gio   What?

Mirko   I sucked.

Gio   No you didn't.

Mirko   Did you see it, the school show?

Gio   The *musical comedy.*

Mirko   What the fuck was it called?

Gio   *The lion* –

Mirko *and* **Gio** (*together*)   – *and the grateful mouse.*

Gio   It was cute 'cause you had all those –

Mirko   Claws?

Gio   No, those things on your arms and legs.

Mirko   Oh. The legwarmers.

Gio   They looked really cool.

Mirko   They made me sweat.

Gio   Do you know who I am?

A pause.

Mirko   I think so.

Gio   You do?

Mirko   You're famous.

Gio   Famous.

Mirko   Your picture's all over the news.

Gio   Which one?

Mirko   You're on a balcony wearing a striped t-shirt, next to a kind of pinwheel.

Gio   I had a spot on my left cheek in that picture!

Mirko   They told everyone to share it, on Instagram, TikTok, even Facebook.

Gio   Shit.

Mirko   They say it's important that everyone . . . *mobilises.*

Gio   Wow.

Mirko   They're not sure if you ran away by yourself or if someone . . .

Gio   . . . what?

Mirko   There's this note –

Gio   They found it?

Mirko   Yeah. In which you told your mum that you were spending the night with the parish youth club.

Gio   I needed to buy some time.

Mirko   . . .

Gio   Before everyone started looking for me. I got the idea from the disappearance of these two girls in Feltre, outside Belluno.

Mirko   Uhm, well your mum started to get suspicious.

Gio   I bet she rang the school and found out I was absent. She can use her brain when she chooses to.

A pause.

Mirko   Anyway . . . *of course* I know who you are. Half of Italy knows who you are.

Gio   Yeah but . . . do you remember me from the show? (*A beat.*) I was in it too.

Mirko   Really?

Gio   I played the North Star.

Mirko   Oh, you were like –

Gio   Yup.

Mirko   Sorry. I can't remember all the stars, there were so many.

Gio   The whole galaxy.

Mirko   So you played a star in the –

Gio   The North Star.

Mirko   I didn't think there was a *North* Star.

Gio   It's real, you know.

Mirko   I know, I know, I meant, I didn't think we had a North Star *in the show,* I thought you were all just stars.

Gio   By the way, it was pretty dangerous putting all those lightbulbs on us, we could have got an electric shock and died.

Mirko (*studying* **Gio** *more closely*)   Did we talk once?

Gio   Yes.

Mirko   That day.

Gio   With the hailstorm.

Mirko   After rehearsal.

Gio   Yup.

Mirko   Fucking hell! That was you.

Gio   You asked me for an umbrella.

Mirko   Did I?

Gio   It was hailing.

Mirko   . . .

Gio   And I lent it to you.

A pause.

Mirko   I don't remember *that*.

Gio   You said that the hailstones were as big as rocks and they might make a hole in my umbrella. I told you not to worry, that I was wearing my hoodie anyway, so you borrowed my umbrella. You were supposed to come to my classroom at the end of the hallway the next day. To give it back. But you didn't.

A pause.

Mirko   Did you know it was me? That *I* was *me*, like –

Gio   Oh yeah . . .

Mirko   But I was all bundled up in my coat that day, all –

Gio   I could still see your eyes. I mean, your face –

Mirko   The boy I talked to the day of the hailstorm was the boy who –

Gio   Disappeared?

Mirko   . . .

Gio   Is that what they say? That I disappeared?

Mirko   Well, you *did* disappear.

Gio   What else do they say?

Mirko   That you were wearing jeans, the day you . . .

Gio   Disappeared?

Mirko   And a grey jumper with two white stripes on the sleeves.

Mirko *realises that* **Gio** *is still wearing that same outfit.*

Gio   I did actually bring a change of clothes.

Mirko   They also say that you might have 'met a horrible end.'

Gio   And are they upset?

Mirko   Who?

Gio   Everyone.

Mirko   What do you think?

Gio   Dunno.

Mirko   Of course they are.

Gio   What else do they say? That I have a few bolts loose?

Mirko   Screws.

Gio   That I have a few screws loose?

Mirko   I mean, you are . . . *peculiar.*

Gio   Because I mind my own business? Because I don't like to show my hands? That's just because I bite my nails. Bitten nails are disgusting.

Mirko   Says who?

Gio   What, do you like them?

Mirko   Tell me who says that biting your nails is disgusting.

Gio   Everyone. Kevin. One time he shouted that if I gave him a hundred euro he'd let me bite his nails too.

Mirko   Can we stop talking about Kevin?

Gio   You're friends with him, aren't you?

Mirko   Anyway, a shy person can be much more interesting, because they have a lot to say but you might not know it because they like, keep it inside. Also, at some point shyness goes away.

A pause.

Gio   When?

Mirko   Whenever. It's like, you decide you want something, and that thing happens.

Gio   Maybe you're right.

Mirko   Do you know why the little plant managed to grow through the rock?

Gio   What plant?

Mirko   Like, *the* little plant, it's a kind of symbol, do you know why it managed to grow through the rock?

Gio *shakes his head 'no'.*

Mirko   Because it didn't know it was impossible.

Gio   Oh.

Mirko   I saw that in a book. It's, like, inspiring.

Gio   Right.

Mirko   I can lend it to you if you want.

Gio   Can you bring it to me?

A pause.

Mirko   Yeah, I can bring it to you.

Gio   You read a lot of books?

Mirko   Mostly self-help books. About real-life stuff. Well, I don't actually read them, I look them up on Booktok.

Gio   . . .

Mirko   Because I don't want to miss out. After graduation, I don't want to become like Kevin, or Zippo, or Alex. I won't let other people decide for me. I'll use my own head. I don't want to end up like the petrol station guy.

Gio   Why?

Mirko   You know him?

Gio   Everyone knows him.

Mirko   Well, they say he used to be rich, very rich.

Gio   Are you sure?

Mirko   And at some point . . . boom, he was poor. He was forced to work at the petrol station. He didn't play his cards right. I don't want to end up like that. I want –

Gio   To play your cards right.

Mirko   Of course, don't you?

Gio   I don't know. I still have my whole life ahead of me. Even if the village thinks I met a horrible end.

A pause.

Mirko   Why did you run away?

Gio   Didn't you see my TikTok?

Mirko   What TikTok?

Gio   If you see it you'll understand. Didn't they show it on the news?

Mirko   I don't think so.

Gio   Watch it.

Mirko   Okay.

Gio   And tell me how it's doing.

Mirko   . . .

Gio   How many views.

Mirko   . . .

Gio   I can't check it from here. I didn't bring my phone, otherwise they'd track me down. 'Cause of signal. They find you in a second. I had to smash it with a rock.

Mirko   Sick.

Gio   The guy who killed that girl in Brembate di Sopra was discovered because of the cell towers.

Mirko   Who?

Gio   You haven't heard of it? The Brembate di Sopra murder! I'm obsessed with all that.

Mirko   With murders?

Gio   And kidnappings. And disappearances. All sorts of mysteries. Did you know that every little village in Italy has its own famous crime?

Mirko   What's ours?

Gio   We don't have one.

Mirko   . . .

Gio   Yet.

A pause.

I found this place because of Kevin. Last year. This one time
he and the others were chasing me through the woods. You
know how they chase me sometimes? I'm not a fast runner,
but I'm clever, and I'm good at finding little hiding places
and squeezing inside, so I found this hole. I stayed here for
hours, like five or six, and eventually . . . I realised that you
could actually live here. It's nice, even though it's cold. Well,
after a few hours I left and I forgot all about it. But then that
thing happened . . .

Mirko   What thing?

Gio   The thing in the music room.

Mirko   Oh.

Gio   I remembered this cave and figured I would . . .
move here.

Mirko   Shit.

Gio   I started stealing things from my house to bring here.
Four blankets, two sets of bedsheets, twenty-four bottles of
water, a pen and a notebook, a first-aid kit, some ibuprofen
and some magazines.

Mirko (*reading the title*)   'Crime Magazine.'

Gio   It's my favourite.

Mirko   Sure.

Gio   I stole a little bit at a time, so nobody noticed. The only
thing is, I miscalculated my provisions. I basically only have
two tins of meat left. I stole them from our kitchen. I know

how to make them last for ages though. I researched it. After you go two days without food, your glycogen stores run out and your body adapts, basically it starts feeding you with whatever's already in it. Like fat. It feeds you with your own fat. You can go up to fifteen or twenty days without food, you know, and only then do you start doing permanent damage to your system. (**Mirko** *starts feeling uneasy*.) If you're also dehydrated then it's a bigger issue, your toenails turn black and your nails too, and your lips –

Mirko   You think it's dark outside?

Gio   Does my breath stink?

Mirko   The days are getting shorter.

Gio   Must be around eight.

Mirko   Fuck. (*He checks his phone*.) Shit, I'm at six per cent.

Gio   The torch drains the battery.

Mirko   I'm going.

Gio   Mirko . . . don't tell anyone I'm here.

Mirko   You know my name.

Gio   I beg you. Don't tell anyone I'm here.

Mirko   . . .

Gio   I trust you.

A pause.

Mirko   Okay.

Gio   It's my secret.

Mirko   Okay.

Gio   Now it's yours, too.

Mirko   Okay.

Gio   It's nice to have a secret.

A pause.

Mirko   It's fucking cold. I'm going.

Gio   Will you come back to visit me?

Mirko   What?

Gio   Will you come back to visit me?

Mirko   Yeah, okay.

Gio   Promise.

Mirko   Alright.

Gio   What if you don't?

Mirko   I said I will.

Gio *frantically opens two tins and empties them on the ground.*

The food gets mixed up with the soil and mud.

Mirko   The fuck are you doing?

Gio   My last two tins. Now you have to come back. Or I die.

Blackout.

Scene Two

A few days later.

On the ground, a shopping bag full of groceries.

Gio *is dirtier.*

Mirko *is decorating the room with a string of fairy lights.*

Mirko   Lithium batteries.

Gio   Oh.

Mirko   They last forever.

Gio   Cool.

Gio *looks through the groceries.*

Mirko   I hope you like borlotti beans.

Gio   Are they the red ones?

Mirko   Yeah, well, there's a bit of everything. All tinned stuff. I brought you a tin opener too. If you mix everything together you can make a kind of salad. Or soup, if you blend everything, but I don't know if you have a, a –

Gio *opens a tin and starts eating voraciously with his hands.*

Mirko   There's cutlery too, if you want.

Gio *keeps stuffing his face.*

Gio   You didn't let anyone see you, right?

Mirko   No, Gio, nobody . . .

Gio   What if someone followed you here?

Mirko   I was careful.

Gio   That's not the point! They could find me, Mirko. Any minute.

Mirko   . . .

Gio   Right?

Mirko   Sure, Gio. What do you want me to say?

Gio *suddenly changes the subject.*

Gio   Did you watch my TikTok?

Mirko   I did, yeah.

Gio   And . . .?

Mirko   I heard they want to take it down. Don't ask me why.

Gio   How many views does it have?

Mirko   Guess.

Gio   Hmmm . . . . A thousand?

Mirko   Eight hundred thousand.

Gio   Are you kidding?

Mirko   Eight hundred thousand and something.

Gio   Thank God that spot was gone when I filmed it!

Mirko   Gio –

Gio   Eight hundred thousand views! That's more than the True Crime Queen gets! So then, they have to pay me, TikTok has to pay me!

Mirko   Gio, I wanted to tell you that –

Gio   Exactly eight hundred thousand?

Mirko   I saw your mum on TV.

Gio   Oh.

Mirko   Her eyes were all red, her hair was all –

Gio   I bet she didn't even get her hair done.

Mirko   What?

Gio   The whole of Italy will see her grey roots. Gross.

Mirko   Gio.

Gio   My dad?

Mirko   I didn't see him –

Gio   Of course.

Mirko   You know who's really upset? Debbie.

Gio   Debbie.

Mirko   Yeah, Debbie.

Gio   She was on TV too?

Mirko   No, on Insta. She's been your best friend since primary school, right?

Gio Is that what she's saying?

Mirko Isn't it true?

Gio A few years ago someone wrote *dog* on her backpack. So she came over to me. *Hey, you know they wrote 'dog' on my backpack? Well they wrote 'freak' on your PE kit, WE ARE DESTINED TO BE FRIENDS!* That's how Debbie became my friend. Debbie. That dog. But I told her, you know, I told her *Debbie, we are not friends. We are simply . . .* (*melodramatic*) *trapped in the same cage*.

Mirko You're weird.

Gio See?

Mirko What?

Gio You think so too.

Mirko People are suffering because of you.

A pause.

They're worried. They think organ traffickers shipped your kidneys to the ends of the earth and threw your body in a dump. (**Gio** *laughs*.) Or that some maniac skinned you alive, cut you into pieces and stuffed you in his freezer. (**Gio** *laughs*.) They're freaking out, Gio. Do you understand?

A pause. **Gio** *stops laughing.*

Gio They'll get over it.

Mirko They're crying for you.

Gio It's scientifically proven that it's impossible to cry *for* someone. We only cry for ourselves.

A pause.

Mirko That man.

Gio What man?

Mirko The petrol station guy.

Gio   Right.

Mirko   The bald guy who works at the petrol station –

Gio   Yeah, I get it.

Mirko   They found him wandering the vineyard at night. Looking for you.

Gio   He was drunk.

Mirko   Did you know him?

Gio   Kind of.

Mirko   They're saying he kidnapped you. They saw you with him. In the village. At least twice. Walking along the river, and also having ice cream by the village hall. They want to, like, interrogate him, arrest him, I don't really know. Is it true that . . . you hung out with him?

Gio   Sometimes.

Mirko   Like?

Gio   Those two times . . . and a couple more. He asked me questions. He has terrible breath. It stinks of wine . . . not really wine, more like rotten grapes. His hands stink of petrol. Obviously.

Mirko   They say he's a *paedophile*.

A pause.

Gio   I don't think so. Paedophiles *like* kids. He wouldn't even touch me. That *good for nothing*.

A long pause.

On to more serious things . . . Did the new season of *Stranger Things* come out?

Mirko (*suddenly*)   NOW YOU LISTEN TO ME, DICKHEAD! Why the fuck did you run away, if you knew you were going to make such a mess? The police are looking for you, the emergency services, there's volunteers, over a hundred and thirty people. They even brought in these special dogs all the way from the Netherlands. All because of your stupid plan.

Gio   It's *your* plan too, now. You're an accomplice.

Mirko   It's your plan, okay? *Your* plan. Maybe I should go to the police and tell them that I found you in this fucking hole where you've been hiding for no good reason. I mean, without any . . . why?

Gio   Because if I go back to school they'll make me lick the floor.

A pause.

With my tongue.

Mirko   . . .

Gio   They did it once, they can do it again.

Mirko   Okay.

Gio   They want to do it again.

Mirko   . . .

Gio   They made me lick the floor.

Mirko   . . .

Gio   Do you know what the floor tastes like?

Mirko   . . .

Gio   I do.

A pause.

The music room wasn't made for that. It was made to listen to Vivaldi, Schubert, to sing Jeff Buckley's *Hallelujah,* not to lick the dust and the dirt. Nobody should ever lick it, that floor, nobody in the world *ever.* I had to brush my teeth a thousand times and rinse with mouthwash because the taste wouldn't go away. (*A beat.*) If you get the chance, tell them

I'd like them to play Jeff Buckley's *Hallelujah* at the church in my honour. I love that song. (*Looks at his hands.*) Shit. I'm all dirty.

Mirko *pulls out some napkins from the grocery bag and starts cleaning* **Gio**'s *hands.*

Mirko (*wiping* **Gio**'s *hands*)   I get it now.

Gio   What?

Mirko   You're a zero-zero.

Gio   That doesn't sound good.

Mirko   Zero-zeros are the hardest to motivate.

Gio   Motivate?

Mirko   Zero-zeros are people who think of themselves and the world around them as nothing, like, everything is a zero to them. That's why you told everyone to go fuck themselves and came to live down here.

Gio   I never thought of it like that.

Mirko   You have to believe in yourself.

Gio   I have to believe . . .

Mirko   In yourself.

Gio   And how do I do that?

Mirko   There are three steps. Step one: focus on what you've already achieved.

Gio   Like what?

Mirko   Like how far you've come.

Gio   Underground?

Mirko   How many people could accomplish that?

Gio   Oh.

Mirko   You have a personality. You're . . . nice.

Gio   Nice?

Mirko   You're funny.

Gio   In a good way?

Mirko   I wish I was as funny as you.

Gio   Yeah right.

Mirko   Step two: establish concrete goals.

Gio   Like what?

Mirko   Something achievable.

Gio   Like, not dying of hunger or thirst.

Mirko   Right.

Gio   Or finding a way to make this place not stink.

Mirko   I'll bring you an air freshener next time.

Gio   Or managing to hide out here for the rest of my days.

Mirko   Seriously?

Gio   What?

Mirko   You're planning to stay down here . . . forever?

Gio   Why not?

Mirko   Well, I don't know –

Gio   You think the outside is better?

Mirko   It's sunny.

Gio   During the day.

Mirko   It's so humid down here.

Gio   Nobody wants anything.

Mirko   There's nobody here.

Gio   Nobody makes you do anything. In the dark you can be whatever you want. Everything. Or nothing. (*A beat*.) Then when you come, I can turn on these little lights.

Mirko   Thanks.

Gio   What's step number three?

Mirko   Talk to yourself.

Gio   I do that all the time.

Mirko   I know that you're strong, deep down.

Gio   Thank you.

Mirko   You're a warrior.

Gio (*he looks at himself*)   I'm all dirty.

Mirko   They're the marks of a warrior.

Gio *smiles, walks over to* **Mirko**.

Gio *hugs* **Mirko**, *holding him tight*.

Mirko *stiffens*. **Gio** *keeps holding him*.

After a few seconds, **Mirko** *returns the hug*.

Gio   I'm not *that* dirty.

Mirko   No worries.

Gio *kisses* **Mirko** *on the cheek*. **Mirko** *pushes him off immediately*.

A long pause.

Gio   Did that gross you out?

A pause.

Gio   It's not mud, it's just a bit of –

Mirko   Yeah, yeah.

Gio   Of soil.

Mirko   Yeah.

Gio   It comes off.

Gio *moves towards* **Mirko** *again to brush the dirt off him, but* **Mirko** *steps back.*

Gio   Did that gross you out?

Mirko   No, no, it's just soil.

Gio   No, I mean the other thing. Did *that* gross you out?

Mirko   Nothing fucking grossed me out!

Gio   Okay.

A pause.

When are you coming back?

Mirko   I live by the motorway, must be like five kilometres from here, six even. Seven, considering you have to walk across the woods. Plus, evenings are hard for me. Tomorrow I have choir, Friday I have training . . .

Gio   Come on Friday. Tell your parents you're going to training and come here instead.

A pause.

Did you say there was cutlery?

Mirko   . . .

Gio   Metal or plastic?

Gio *searches through the grocery bag. He pulls out a knife and uses it to cut off a little piece of his jumper sleeve.*

Mirko   The fuck are you doing?

Gio *hands it to* **Mirko**.

Gio   Take it.

Mirko   Why?

Gio   Tell everyone you found it.

Mirko   What?

Gio   While you were hanging around. In the woods. Not around here, though. Say that you found it . . . in the San Luca woods. You'll throw off the investigation. They'll never find me.

Mirko   . . .

Gio   San Luca is fifteen kilometres away.

Mirko   But what if they find out –

Gio   Nobody will find out.

Mirko   Who am I supposed to talk to?

Gio   Start with the Carabinieri. Then I'm sure the media will be all over it.

Mirko   What?

Gio   When that girl from Avetrana disappeared her uncle found her mobile phone without a SIM card or battery and he got tons of TV interviews. Same with the guy who found the backpack of that boy who went missing in the Trentino woods.

Mirko   Why would I give a shit about being interviewed?

Gio   What do you mean?! You'll get tons of new followers. Maybe you'll become the boss and overthrow Kevin's dictatorship. Or maybe, wait, wait . . . Mirko, is there a girl that you like?

Mirko   What's that got to do with it?

Gio   Sara.

Mirko   The fuck do you know.

Gio   Everyone knows.

Mirko   Nobody knows. You can't tell!

Gio   Oh, so it's true!

Mirko   Stop!

Gio   Don't you think that finding a piece of the jumper of the boy who disappeared will be a good way to make her notice you?

Mirko   She already notices me.

Gio   Yes, but if you go on TV you'll be the connection between the two worlds. He who knows the Upside Down, and can descend into Hades if he so chooses. You'll be *the chosen one.*

One of the lightbulbs flickers, making a sizzling sound.

You sure they last forever?

Blackout.

Scene Three

Friday night.

The fairy lights are on.

Mirko *is dressed for his football training.*

Mirko *and* **Gio** *are in the middle of a heated conversation.*

They're in high spirits, having fun with each other.

Mirko   I couldn't even move my head or anything, so at one point I was like, *excuse me, am I allowed to breathe?!* Because if I moved, even a little bit, to the right or to the left, then I'd be out of the . . .

Gio   Frame!

Mirko   Exactly. Then they put a microphone on my belt, you know, for the audio, and we tested it too. There was a sound guy!

Gio   Wow.

Mirko   And I said to the whole of Italy . . . (**Gio** *laughs*.) . . . well, to the whole world . . . (**Gio** *laughs harder*) . . . that I found a piece of your jumper in the San Luca woods.

Gio   And they believed it?

Mirko   Of course!

Gio   Awesome!

Mirko   The journalist nodded at everything I said. They did an edit like shot reverse shot. And it was so funny 'cause she had all this makeup on and was dressed all fancy, wearing like a suit, but she had trainers on! Because who gives a fuck, right, they don't show her shoes anyway . . .

Gio   What else did you say?

Mirko   Nothing really, it was all over so quickly, you know, less than a minute. They asked me if we're friends.

Gio   And?

Mirko   I said yeah. That we knew each other . . . I mean, we know each other . . .

Gio   If Debbie says she's my friend, you can definitely say it.

Mirko   Exactly.

Gio   And Sara?

Mirko   Sara what?

Gio   Did she see you on TV?

Mirko   Look, if you're going to be a pain in the ass, I'm leaving.

Gio   I thought you came back to fill me in.

Mirko   Yeah, but not about Sara –

Gio   Yes about Sara. I want to know about Sara.

A pause.

Mirko   . . . I have to make sense of my feelings.

Gio   Wow.

Mirko   So I don't string her along.

Gio   So she loves you?

Mirko   Well, 'loves'. She's into me.

Gio   How do you know?

Mirko   She's been liking all my posts for days. And replying to my stories.

Gio   Perfect.

Mirko   This morning we had Assembly in the great hall and her friend wouldn't stop staring at me.

Gio   What?

Mirko   Her friend.

Gio   Shit, so maybe her friend likes you.

Mirko   No, no, Sara's just too shy to look at me. So her friend looks at me for her.

Gio   Oh.

Mirko   And I obviously look back at her.

Gio   So . . . her friend looks at you and you look at Sara?

Mirko   No, no, I look at her friend!

Gio   So then she'll think you like her friend!

Mirko   Even better! If you like a girl, flirt with her friend.

Gio   What?!

Mirko   Everyone knows that.

Gio   If I liked a girl, I would flirt with that girl.

Mirko   Well, *you* wouldn't –

Gio   Obviously.

Mirko   There are three rules –

Gio   Again?

Mirko   The three rules of seduction.

Gio   Rule number one is –

Mirko   To flirt with her friend. Rule number two is: if she's pretty, tell her she's smart and if she's smart –

Gio   – tell her she's pretty.

Mirko   Even if you have to lie.

Gio   And rule number three?

Mirko   Never appear inexperienced.

Gio   Interesting.

Mirko   Girls like to feel that you're in control, that you know where to put your hands.

Gio   And how do you show them that?

Mirko   . . .

Gio   Because it'll get to that, right? Once you've *made sense of your feelings*. You'll find yourself alone with her in the garage, or in a bush or in a closet –

Mirko   . . . maybe somewhere a bit nicer . . .

Gio   Or here? How nice would it be if it was here?! I think this cave is splendid for *fucking!*

Mirko   Gio!

Gio   Naked bodies on the damp ground.

Mirko   Yeah, I don't think so.

Gio   How will you show her that you know what you're doing?

Mirko   Don't you worry, I know what to do.

Gio   Can you teach me?

Mirko   Are you planning on bringing someone down here?

Gio   You're a virgin.

A pause.

You've never had sex.

Mirko   . . .

Gio   I've never done it either.

Mirko   How the fuck would you –

Gio   From the computer room. One day, I got the laptop you'd just used. I went on Google. Recent searches: *how do you have sex?* I thought – that's so cute, he's never done it, he's doing his research. Second search: *how to please a woman.* He's awesome, he's worried about her, like, he wants to *please* her. Third search: *sexually transmitted diseases.* Very prudent on your part. My grandma would really like you.

A pause.

Mirko   Fuck you.

Gio   Who do you like?

Mirko   Fuck you.

Gio   Who's a girl that you like? Other than Sara.

Mirko   What, in what –

Gio   Who would you like to . . .

Mirko   *Fuck?*

Gio   Yes.

A brief pause. **Mirko** *thinks about it.*

Mirko   You mean from school or –

Gio   Whoever.

Mirko   Emily Ratajkowski.

Gio   And you'd like to –

Mirko   Yeah.

Gio   In what ways?

Mirko   I DON'T FUCKING KNOW!

A pause.

Gio   I like superheroes.

A pause.

Mirko   That's cool.

Gio   I like picturing them naked.

Mirko (*a brief pause*)   Marvel ones or . . .?

Gio   All of them.

Mirko   Okay.

Gio   Naked, but with socks on.

Mirko   . . .

Gio   I like to picture them wearing sports socks. White spongy socks.

A pause.

Mirko   I wear those too.

Gio   White?

Mirko   With two blue stripes.

Gio   Are you wearing them now?

Mirko   The fuck do you care.

Gio   Okay.

A pause.

Gio   I'd like to kiss Green Lantern on the mouth.

Mirko   That's fucked up.

Gio   Bite his chin. And his shoulders. Then run my fingers along his shoulder blades. Gently. And his ears, too.

Mirko   And if he strikes you with his green ray?

Gio   Even better. I'd let him take me and do whatever he wants with me.

Mirko   . . . Okay.

Gio   It's not my fault I like body parts.

Mirko   Body parts . . . are beautiful.

Gio   Which ones do you like?

Mirko   On girls?

Gio   On bodies.

Mirko   . . . Hands?

Gio   Do you like mine? (*Shows him his hands.*) Sorry about my nails.

Mirko   No worries.

Gio   What are they like?

Mirko   They're okay. Normal. Soft.

Gio   How can you tell?

Mirko   I don't know, they look soft.

Gio   You can touch them.

Mirko   Why?

Gio   Touch them. If you feel anything, you know, *sharp*, it's, well . . .

Mirko and **Gio** *clumsily interlace hands.*

The boys are very close to each other now.

Gio   Feel anything sharp?

Mirko   Not really.

Gio   Am I cute or gross?

Mirko   You're . . . well-proportioned. You're cute.

Gio   Are you saying that because of rule number two? If they're smart, tell them they're cute?

Mirko   No, come on.

Gio   Okay.

Mirko   Now what?

Gio   Try.

Mirko   To do what?

Gio   To give me a . . .

Mirko   I don't know.

Gio   No one can see us.

Mirko   Come on.

Gio   What?

Mirko   I don't –

Gio   So with Sara you'll be more –

Mirko   Experienced?

Gio   Experienced, yeah.

Mirko   I don't know if, if it's for me, I mean.

Gio   But this isn't you. And this isn't me. It's a *simulation*. Like a game. It's dark. We're everyone and no one.

A pause.

Mirko   What did you mean? When you said you wanted Green Lantern to take you and do whatever he wants with you?

Gio *suddenly kisses* **Mirko**.

Gio   What was that like?

Mirko   You taste like canned meat.

Gio   It was beans.

Mirko   Beans . . . .

Gio   Borlotti beans.

Mirko   Yeah.

Gio   . . . good?

Mirko   I don't know.

Gio *kisses him again*.

Gio   Now?

Mirko   Sauce. Tomato sauce.

Gio   What else?

Mirko   Long-life milk.

Gio   What else?

Mirko   . . . Mint?

Gio   That's how I taste.

Mirko   Good to know.

Gio   Can I do that again?

Mirko   No. But I can.

Mirko *kisses* **Gio**.

Gio   Do whatever you want.

They smile at each other and kiss again.

Blackout.

Scene Four

Ten days later, maybe a little longer.

Pitch-black darkness.

Gio *is alone. He's sleeping like an animal, curled up on the ground, feral, surrounded by more empty tins and rubbish than before. He's the dirtiest he's ever been.*

Mirko *enters and spots him. He's angry.*

Mirko   Jesus Christ.

Gio (*groggy*)   Who's there?

Mirko   Police!

Gio   What?

Mirko   I threw two rocks down, no answer. (**Gio** *doesn't know what to say.*) Fucking rock signal – what if you die?

Gio   I won't die.

Mirko   Great.

Gio   What's wrong with you?

Mirko   It stinks in here.

Gio   I'll just open up the windows.

Mirko   And it's dark as shit.

Mirko *finds the fairy lights and switches them on. Many of them have burned out. He looks at them.*

Shit.

He looks around at the piles of empty tins and rubbish.

Mirko   Look at all this rubbish, it's a fucking mess.

Gio *studies* **Mirko**.

Gio   Where have you been?

Mirko   Nowhere.

Gio   You didn't come for twelve days.

Mirko   You counted.

Gio   In my notebook.

Mirko   Sooner or later you'll lose track of time.

Gio   Your hair's longer.

Mirko   It's the first thing that happens to people who get stuck on a desert island, or trapped under a sheet of ice, they lose track of time.

Gio   I won't.

Mirko   Why were you sleeping?

Gio   Don't you sleep at night?

Mirko   Oh, it's night is it?

Gio   Must be five, six in the morning.

Mirko   It's four in the afternoon, Gio, it's a nice Saturday afternoon. You know it's Saturday, right?

Gio   You're making fun of me.

Mirko   Get your ass outside and look.

A pause.

Gio   Although, really, maybe it's Tuesday and you say it's Saturday, maybe it's nighttime and you say it's day, maybe you made up my mum crying, the TV, Debbie, the vans full of journalists. Maybe there's a zombie apocalypse and you're not telling me anything. Maybe they haven't even noticed that I disappeared. Which would be much worse than a zombie apocalypse. I mean, if I didn't trust you, I'd be worried. But I trust you. So I'm not. Welcome back.

A pause.

Mirko   Clean yourself up.

Gio   Jesus, you don't show up for days and then you –

Mirko   And use the pillows, shit.

Gio   Yessir.

Mirko   At night, though, not in the day!

Gio   Alright!

Mirko   Go and get them.

Gio (*going to get the pillows*)   Did you celebrate?

Mirko   What?

Gio   Your birthday.

Mirko   How did you know it was my birthday?

Gio   Did you celebrate?

Mirko   Not this year.

Gio   Why?

Mirko   I didn't feel like it.

Gio   Why?

Mirko   BECAUSE! (*A pause.*) Give me something to sit on.

A pause.

Gio   Okay. (*Rifles through the magazines.*)

Mirko   Not one of those. (**Gio** *looks at him.*) Something more comfortable.

Gio   The blankets? (**Mirko** *doesn't look convinced.*) I can make a pile.

Mirko   Whatever.

Gio   Okay.

Gio *pulls out the blankets, makes a little pile, trying to make it as neat and comfortable as possible.*

Mirko   The pillows, too.

Gio *adds two pillows to the pile.*

Mirko *sits on it. Stretches out his legs.*

He stares at **Gio** *for a few seconds.*

Mirko   Shoes.

Gio *stares at him.*

Mirko   Shoes.

Gio   What?

Mirko   Go on.

Gio   You want me to . . .

Mirko   I'm tired, I walked all the way here.

Gio *looks at him for a few seconds longer.*

Then he kneels at his feet.

Mirko   Good.

Gio *reaches for* **Mirko***'s feet.*

Mirko   No. One at a time.

Gio *uses both hands to untie the laces of* **Mirko***'s right shoe, then he gently pulls it off.* **Mirko** *is wearing spongy white socks.*

Mirko   You like them?

Gio   Yes.

Mirko   Do the other one.

Gio *takes* **Mirko***'s other shoe off.*

He looks at **Mirko** *for a few seconds.*

Gio   What now?

Mirko *takes a small packet from his pocket and throws it to* **Gio***.*

Mirko   Wet wipes.

Gio   Thanks.

Mirko   Use them.

Gio   Okay.

Gio *starts cleaning himself roughly with the wipes.*

Mirko   Everywhere, properly.

Gio   Okay.

Mirko   Take one.

Mirko *throws* **Gio** *a pack of gum.* **Gio** *grabs it, pulls out a stick of gum and starts chewing.*

Mirko   Your hair.

Gio *shakes out his hair, and a small cloud of soil and dust fills the air.*

Mirko   Okay.

Gio   Now?

Mirko   Get naked.

Gio   Get –

Mirko   Naked.

Gio *studies* **Mirko** *for a few seconds.*

Gio   Can I . . . turn –

Mirko   Yeah. Yeah. Turn off the lights.

Blackout.

Scene Five

A half hour later.

Mirko *and* **Gio**, *lying close together, wrapped up in blankets, bedsheets and pillows.*

Mirko *is showing* **Gio** *some photos on his Reflex camera screen. The boys are lit only by the light from the camera.*

Mirko   Look at that colour, it's greener than the leaf.

Gio *shifts as if feeling pain somewhere.*

Mirko   Are you in pain?

Gio   Don't worry. (*Goes back to looking at the camera screen.*) What about this one?

Mirko   That is a *painted lady*, commonly known as a . . .?

Gio   Butterfly.

Mirko   Right.

Gio   You didn't touch it, right?

Mirko   Course not.

Gio   If you touch it, it dies.

Mirko   I know.

Gio   You're good.

Mirko   Thank you. I want to study photography after school.

Gio   Now will you tell me what's wrong?

Mirko   What?

Gio   Earlier. You came in here like a fury. Giving me orders and –

Mirko   I thought you'd like it.

Gio   I'd like to know why you're so angry.

Mirko   The world is shit.

Gio   Not the world of insects.

Mirko   Not the world of insects, no, but the world of people, yeah.

A pause.

Mirko   Kevin saw my interview on TV.

Gio   And?

Mirko   You know that thing I said to the journalist?

Gio   About the piece of my jumper?

Mirko   No . . . that we're, that the two of us are, like, friends. They didn't like . . .

Gio   Who?

Mirko   Kevin – the others too, but mostly Kevin – they thought we were friends before, like *before-before*, before you disappeared. Like maybe there was something between us . . .

Gio   . . . what?

Mirko   . . .

Gio   What?

Mirko   Something.

Gio   Oh.

Mirko   He doesn't know shit. He convinced Zippo too, and Alex, all the guys in the choir, the ones in my class, you know what Kevin's like, everyone believes him. (*A beat.*) None of them came to my fucking party.

Gio   So you did have a party!

Mirko   Not even Sara!

Gio   Oh no.

Mirko   Those assholes.

Gio   Yeah.

Mirko   She stopped messaging me.

Gio   I'm sorry.

Mirko   Yeah.

Gio   I'm sorry, I swear.

Mirko   I believe you. It kind of took me by surprise, this stuff –

Gio   I bet.

Mirko   They made a WhatsApp group. Without me. For the first time. It's called *Mirko & Gio are BFFs.*

Gio   That's cute.

Mirko   With the aubergine emoji. The sweat emoji. And the pig emoji.

Gio   All of that fits in the group name?

Mirko   Debbie showed me. She's in it. And I'm not. THEY MADE A MEME OF ME WITH A DICK IN MY MOUTH, FOR FUCK'S SAKE. (*A beat.*) My dad made a massive scene, Gio. He's going to get them into so much shit, you know? He's a lawyer, my dad. He knows how these things work, *this is defamation*, so of course he wants to make them suffer, those dickheads!

Gio   You asked your dad to sue Kevin?

Mirko   Not really. He just, like, found out about the WhatsApp group. And he got pissed at me 'cause I didn't tell him, but like what the fuck was I supposed to tell him?

Gio   Right . . .

Mirko   So yeah. He decided to do something about it.

Gio   Does Kevin know? That your dad wants to like, make trouble for him?

Mirko   I just want the truth to come out, Gio.

Gio   Right.

Mirko   For everyone to know that I have nothing to do with you.

Gio   Right.

Mirko   Right.

A pause.

Gio   Why are they so obsessed with me?

Mirko   I don't know what to tell you . . .

Gio   Two boys can't be –

Mirko   It's not about that –

Gio   So it's about me?

A pause.

Mirko   Everyone goes on about the thing in the woods.

Gio   *The thing in the woods?*

Mirko   The dirty thing in the woods.

Gio   *The dirty thing in the woods?*

Mirko   I don't know what the fuck it is. Kevin and the others talk about it all the time, something that happened ages ago.

Gio   The dirty thing in the woods.

Mirko   That's why they started saying –

Gio   What?

Mirko   That you're weird.

Gio   Because of the dirty –

Mirko   – thing in the woods, the dirty thing in the woods! That's where it all began, that's why they wrote *freak* on your bag, that's why they took you to the music room!

Gio   Okay.

Mirko   I just want my life back, fuck.

Mirko *cries.*

Mirko (*whimpering*)   I don't do dirty things in the woods . . . I don't do dirty things . . .

Gio *lets him vent.*

Gio   I got you a present. For your birthday.

Mirko   You went shopping?

Gio   No, I –

Mirko   Does Amazon deliver here?

Gio   It's a cake. Made of mud.

Mirko   You're nuts.

Gio *gets the cake and presents it to* **Mirko**.

It's a shapeless block of mud with a few things sticking out of it: a toy soldier, a button, a tooth and a coin.

Gio   You can't eat it.

Mirko   I figured.

Gio   I didn't have any candles –

Mirko   Obviously.

Gio   But wait –

Gio *turns on the fairy lights. A good half of them have burned out.*

Mirko   They burned out.

Gio   You like it?

Mirko   What's on it? Or, in it?

Gio   Well. (*He picks up the coin.*) The coin represents money, because you want to play your cards right and not end up like the petrol station guy. Then (*he picks up the button*) the button is for the secret that binds us together. (**Mirko** *looks puzzled.*) You know the saying . . . to be buttoned up, meaning to be secretive. (*Before* **Mirko** *can reply.*) Then (*he picks up the tooth*) . . .

Mirko   Gross.

Gio   It's a tooth.

Mirko   Exactly.

Gio   It represents the fact that you're growing up. And when we grow up, we get our wisdom teeth. And finally (*he picks up the toy soldier*) the soldier. This one doesn't need an explanation, right? I wanted to give you four things that described you.

Mirko   You looked for things that described me?

Gio   Actually, they're the only things I found. In the mud. And then I tried to connect them to you. Like, I did it the other way round. (*A beat.*) Remember when you told me that if you want something enough, eventually that thing happens?

Mirko   Sure.

Gio   I think it's true. Because I really wanted you to show up in my cave. I signed up to the choir for you.

A pause.

Mirko   Could you brush your teeth?

Gio   Does my breath stink?

Mirko   I want to give you a fucking kiss with tongue, Gio.

Gio   And my breath –

Mirko   A bit.

Gio   Can you give me another piece of gum?

Mirko   It's better if you really brush them.

Gio *gets his toothbrush and quickly brushes his teeth with toothpaste and some water from a big plastic bottle.*

Gio   Anyway, I'm glad you calmed down. And that you came back.

Mirko   Yeah.

They kiss.

A deep and intense kiss.

The boys eventually break apart but stay close to each other.

Mirko   When they saw me on TV, everyone *loved* me. But it didn't last. People just forget about everything. Everything! Your story, too.

Gio   . . . What?

Mirko   Nothing, like, they're making peace with it.

Gio   With what?

Mirko   With your disappearance. It's for the best, right? So they'll leave you alone. That's what you wanted, right? To stay down here in peace. Alone. Well, with me coming to visit once in a while.

Gio   What . . . What do you mean they're making peace with it?

Mirko   No, listen, don't take it the wrong way. They're still searching for you, obviously, it's not like they've stopped. But it's not like before. Like they're not talking about you on the news anymore. There's not that many search parties anymore . . . Although they are looking into everyone you chatted with online. All those *men*. Are you sure you were a virgin too?

Gio   There's no more search parties?

Mirko   Gio, people are like that. After a while, they forget. Now they think you're dead. People are dicks, Gio. They're idiots. I really think you had the right idea, hiding down here.

Gio *is deep in thought.*

Gio   You have to go back to the world of the living with something.

Mirko   Like what?

Gio   Something horrifying. This time you have to let others find it.

Mirko   Something horrifying?

Gio   If something horrifying turns up, people will start talking about me again. And those dickheads will leave you alone.

Mirko   . . .

Gio   It's obvious. I'm not the only one who loves True Crime.

Mirko *considers this.*

Mirko   Something big . . .

Gio   Yeah . . .

Mirko   Something scary . . .

Gio   Sure. Are there any new theories on my disappearance?

Mirko   Take your pick: you ran away on your own, you were murdered, some people think you were kidnapped . . .

Gio   Makes sense. I read this article in *Crime Magazine* about Sardinian bandits. They kept their hostages in caves, like this one. And at some point they'd start sending the family little pieces of them: an earlobe, a finger, an amputated limb . . .

Mirko   So you think we could –

Gio   What?

Mirko   Like, could we –

Gio   It's an idea.

Mirko   If you agree –

Gio   Yeah, sure.

Mirko   I could write a note from the kidnappers or –

Gio   Yeah.

Mirko   What else?

Gio   I'm not sure.

Mirko   Can you think of anything?

Gio   I don't know.

Mirko   What if I cut . . .

Gio   A lock of my hair?

Mirko   Yeah, exactly.

Gio   Yeah.

Mirko   Yeah.

Gio   We can cut a whole chunk if you want.

Mirko   But hair might be, I don't know, we might need something more . . .

Gio   . . . like?

Mirko   Do earlobes grow back?

Gio   You want to –

Mirko   I don't know.

Gio   You want to cut my –

Mirko   I don't know, I was just thinking of something powerful.

Gio   Oh.

Mirko   But if you don't want to –

Gio   You think it'll hurt?

Mirko   I don't know, it shouldn't.

Gio   Maybe we should freeze it first.

Mirko   Oh.

Gio   Use some freeze spray. I saw it on TV.

Mirko   Oh. You have some?

Gio   No. I don't think so . . .

Mirko   And we can't do it without that?

A long pause.

Gio   You want to use the tin opener?

Mirko   How, I don't –

Gio   The little wheel is sharp.

A pause.

Mirko   Okay.

Mirko *gets the tin opener and brings it over to* **Gio**.

Mirko   Which one?

Gio   What do you mean?

Mirko   Which lobe?

Gio   The lobe!

Mirko   There are two.

Gio   The right one or the left one.

Mirko   No, there's a top one and a bottom one.

Gio   Isn't the lobe just the bottom one?

Mirko   Well, no, there's a top lobe and a bottom lobe.

Gio   Oh. Then I'd say the bottom one.

Mirko   I don't know how to . . . wait, maybe like . . . no, like this.

Gio   The bandits managed it and you can't?

Mirko *slams the tin opener closed with a sharp movement, hitting* **Gio**'s *ear.* **Gio** *yells as his ear starts to bleed.*

Gio   Jesus!

Mirko   Fuck . . .

Gio   God . . .

Mirko   Wait, wait . . .

Mirko *runs to get a rag, hands it to* **Gio** *who uses it to stop the blood flow.*

Gio   Did you cut it?

Mirko   No!

Gio   Shit.

Mirko   It didn't come off, fuck.

Gio   It's fucking bleeding . . .

Mirko   Fuck . . .

Gio   Look at this . . . (*Showing the rag which is now soaked in blood.*)

Mirko   Hold it against your ear.

Gio   Right. (*Holds it to his ear.*) If you look over there . . .

Mirko   Where?

Gio   In the box.

Mirko   Which fucking box!

Gio   Calm down.

Mirko   Where, where, where?

Gio   There!

Mirko (*finding the box*)   Here it is.

Gio   The first-aid kit.

Mirko   Awesome.

Mirko *brings the first-aid kit over to* **Gio**.

Mirko (*rifling through it*)   What do you need, what –

Gio   I don't know . . .

Mirko   I don't fucking know what this stuff is!

Gio   There's some antiseptic.

Mirko   Okay.

Gio   The sterile cotton.

Mirko   Okay.

Gio   Then, I don't know, you can wrap it up with gauze.

Mirko   Okay.

Gio *exposes his bleeding ear.* **Mirko** *looks at him, horrified.*

Gio   Don't be scared.

Mirko *starts dabbing* **Gio**'s *ear with the cotton.*

Gio   Good.

Mirko   Like this?

Gio   Very good.

Mirko   I didn't mean to, Gio, I didn't think it –

Gio   You're doing great.

Mirko   I didn't mean to –

Gio   Don't worry.

Mirko   Maybe I should have washed my hands first.

Gio   It's okay. Can I . . .? (*Lean on* **Mirko**'s *knees.*)

Mirko   Go for it.

Gio *leans his head on* **Mirko**'s *knees.*

Gio   It's not that bad. It's bleeding a lot but the wound isn't deep. You just need to dab it with the antiseptic . . . and the hydrogen peroxide.

Mirko   Okay.

Mirko *tends to* **Gio**'s *wound.*

A brief pause.

Gio   You know. That story. That . . . I don't know how long ago it was. We were ten, I think. You remember Daniel? He lived in the village for a while. He sat next to me in class. One day, I asked him to marry me. He said yes. We met one afternoon, you know that bit off the motorway? And, well, we got married. It was fucking hot, we were wearing these straw hats for shade. There were six or seven kids with us, girls and boys, to be the witnesses. There's usually only two witnesses, but six or seven kids asked us and we didn't want to say no to anyone. I was wearing one of my grandma's lace doilies on my head. As a veil. He put the ring on my finger, a silver ring with a black stone. I got it from my grandma's jewellery box. Before going into the woods, I gave it to Daniel and told him to put it on my finger at the right moment. Then I was going to return it to grandma, 'cause she'd notice if her ring was missing. After the ring, Daniel gave me a kiss on the shoulder and the other kids threw rice at us. That would have been the end of it. Except someone walked by. I don't even remember who. But someone saw us. One of the grown-ups, not one of the kids. They saw us and turned it into something it wasn't. They started spreading this rumour that we were . . . I don't know, masturbating, or doing drugs. The rumour reached everyone and it went down in history as 'the dirty thing in the woods'. I got in massive trouble with my parents. My teachers stopped looking me in the eye. Daniel had to move towns. And I started biting my nails.

Mirko   The bleeding slowed down.

Gio *holds up a spray can he just found inside the first-aid kit.*

Mirko   What's that?

Gio   Freeze spray. Who knew this was in here?

Mirko   You think that –

Gio   We can cut the lobe. Freeze the ear and cut the lobe. Without any pain.

Mirko   Are you . . . sure?

Gio   One clean hit though, okay? Nice and strong.

Mirko   Okay.

Gio   You can use these. (*He holds out some pliers from the kit.*)

Mirko   Better than the tin opener.

Gio   Yeah. Are you happy?

Mirko (*taking the pliers*)   Yeah.

Gio   Yeah. (*He sprays the freeze spray on his injured ear.*) Now I have a frozen ear. Cut.

Mirko *positions the pliers by* **Gio**'s *ear.*

He looks away.

Mirko   Three . . . two . . . one . . .

Just before the pliers touch **Gio**'s *ear . . .*

. . . blackout.

Scene Six

A couple of days later.

Gio *is crouched in a corner, weakened, his ear hurting. He dabs it with a filthy cloth that's already drenched in blood.*

Mirko, *keeping his distance, at the entrance of the cave, his face pale. He's holding a little plastic bag with pharmacy supplies.*

Mirko   Gio.

Gio   My ear . . . it hurts . . .

Mirko   Gio . . .

Gio   There's some white stuff coming out of it.

Mirko   I don't know if it was a good idea.

Gio   What if it's infected?

Mirko   Gio –

Gio   Did you get me more gauze?

Mirko   Yeah, yeah, it's all here, but listen to me for a sec –

Gio   It fucking hurts!

Mirko   They took me to the police station. They asked me a ton of questions. I think they think I did it. They said the jumper thing made them suspicious, and now the ear . . .

Gio   Didn't you leave it behind the petrol station loos?

Mirko   Yeah, but . . . they think maybe I planted it, and I did plant it, and maybe someone saw me . . .

Gio   Like who?

Mirko   I don't fucking know, they didn't say! I don't even know if that's what happened. I bet it was Debbie. She never minds her own business. I didn't do anything. Did I hurt you?!

Gio   No.

Mirko   They're sure of it. They tried everything to make me confess, but confess what, Jesus Christ? They all think that, I don't know, I like, killed you.

Gio   They'll figure out that it's not true, calm down . . .

Mirko   This morning –

Gio   Give me the stuff, Mirko, please –

Mirko   This morning I went to church with my parents. Your mum was a few rows in front of us. At one point she turned and gave me this look . . .

Gio *forcefully grabs* **Mirko***'s wrist.*

Gio   Stop talking.

Mirko   Ouch, Gio, you're . . .

Gio (*staring at* **Mirko**, *challenging him*)   Am I hurting you, Mirko?

A pause.

Mirko   I didn't think it would bleed that much, Gio.

Gio *drops* **Mirko**'s *arm.*

Gio   You have to get them talking about the kidnappers.

Mirko   HOW DO I DO THAT?!

Gio   I'll do it. (*He gets his dirty notebook and a pen.*)

Mirko   The fuck are you doing?

Gio *writes a note, trying to ignore the pain. Just a few words. Then he hands it to* **Mirko**.

Gio   Don't get your fingerprints on it.

Mirko   What did you write?

Gio   '*I'm fine. They're keeping me in a secret location. Stop looking for me. Or they'll hurt me. Gio.*' (*He collapses back down in his corner, dabbing his ear.*) Leave it somewhere they can find it.

Mirko   Why?

Gio   If they believe that I was kidnapped, they'll leave you alone.

Mirko   Gio, that's not going to work. You're holed up down here, you don't know what's going on out there . . .

Gio   Trust me.

Mirko   Gio, if they catch me . . . if they catch you . . . Fuck, this is *much* worse than the WhatsApp group, you get that?

Gio   Leave it somewhere they can find it. A place you'd never normally choose.

Mirko   Okay.

Gio   Don't let them see you.

Mirko   Okay.

Gio   Don't get your fingerprints on it.

Mirko   Okay.

Gio   Don't mess up.

Mirko   I have to go. (*Starts to exit.*)

Gio   How's it going with Kevin?

Mirko   Oh. Everything's okay. He got them to delete that WhatsApp group. And he made a new one. With me in it. Now . . . he respects me.

Gio   Because he thinks you killed me?

Mirko   Yeah.

Gio   He doesn't know shit.

Blackout.

Scene Seven

A few days later.

Mirko *is trying to open a bottle of champagne.*

Gio*'s ear is bandaged up. The wound seems under control.*

The fairy lights are on.

Mirko   Come on, come on, come on.

Gio   Careful –

Mirko (*getting the bottle open*)   No glasses –

Gio   From the bottle.

Mirko   Awesome! (**Mirko** *drinks then passes the bottle to* **Gio**.) How fucking right were you?! You wouldn't believe the shit they came up with . . . the mafia, Satan worshippers, some

people say there's a cannibal in the village . . . (*They laugh*.)
Mothers aren't letting their kids go out by themselves, not
even to the playground! (*They laugh*.) Your mum's stopped
eating.

Gio What do you mean?

Mirko Like, a hunger strike, until they let you go.

Gio Who?

Mirko The kidnappers.

Gio Oh.

Mirko So, she's not eating. I, however, brought you some
nachos. Should we dig in?

Gio If my mum's stopped eating, the situation must be dire.

Mirko Gio. I've never met anyone like you. You are the
most ingenious, smartest and most rebellious little dickhead
on the planet. Well, I don't know about the planet, but
definitely in the village.

Gio Why?

Mirko You said screw this life, you told the whole world to
fuck off. You, you . . . Gio, you have all of my admiration.

Gio But do you care about me?

Mirko What's that got to do with it?

Gio Do you care about me or not?

Mirko Of course.

Gio Me too.

Mirko Okay.

Gio I care about you too.

Mirko Come on.

Gio And that thing you said . . . It goes for me too.

Mirko   What?

Gio   That you've never met anyone like me.

Mirko   Yeah.

Gio   I mean, for you. I mean, I also never met anyone like you.

Gio *hugs* **Mirko***, who doesn't hug him back.*

Gio   Can you hug me properly?

Mirko   My hands are dirty.

Gio   I don't give a shit.

Mirko   Okay.

Mirko *hugs him back.*

A pause.

Gio   Mirko . . .

Mirko   Hmm?

Gio   I've never felt like this.

Mirko   Like what?

Gio   . . . cared for.

Mirko   Okay.

Gio   It makes me feel . . .

Mirko   How?

Gio   *Bigger.*

Mirko   Yeah.

Gio   Kevin and all the others seem so small and . . . harmless.

Mirko   Well, good.

A pause.

Gio You . . . broke me apart and put me back together. You're my carpenter, Mirko, my, I don't know, my architect. You *invented* me. Mirko?

Mirko Yeah?

Gio I thought about it a lot. About staying down here forever. They'd think I was dead. And they'd do all this nice stuff. They'd make a little figurine of me for the church nativity scene, maybe looking like a little angel, and hang me on Joseph and Mary's hut. Which would be an honour, that hut dates back to the 1800s. I would disappear from the world but I would live on forever in that nativity scene, with everyone crying and remembering me. Forever. Or at least at Christmas time. That's what I wanted when I came down here. I disappeared so that I wouldn't disappear. It was silly. I was scared and I ran away. But I'm not anymore. And I want to come out.

Mirko What?

Gio I'm not a zero-zero anymore.

Mirko You want to come out of –

Gio This place.

Mirko But why?

Gio All of this dust . . . this darkness . . .

Mirko But you like the dust and the darkness.

Gio Yeah, but –

Mirko You're a creature of the night, aren't you?

Gio I don't know. I'm a little old to play hide and seek. And I don't want my mum to starve to death.

Mirko She won't starve to death, it's all for show. You know what they're like.

Gio Who?

Mirko   Our parents, they say they love us and then . . .

Gio   Your dad helped you when Kevin was picking on you.

Mirko   Everything is shit out there, Gio. The right thing to do is what you did, leaving all that shit behind once and for all and –

Gio   So why don't you move in here too?

Mirko   What's that got to do with it?

Gio   If you think it's the right thing.

Mirko   But –

Gio   You think it's the smartest thing?

Mirko   Yeah . . .

Gio   So why don't you do it too?

Mirko   Gio.

Gio   We can do whatever we want down here, right?

Mirko   Yeah, but –

Gio   I want to do whatever I want outside. Feel the air again, the sun, eat something good.

Mirko   What would you like?

Gio   I don't know, pizza, for one thing.

Mirko   I'll bring you some.

Gio   That's not the point.

Mirko   I'll get it to you hot, I can bring you all the food you want. I'll figure out a way to get WiFi down here too.

Gio   Thank you. That's so nice. But no. I want to leave. The world is waiting for me.

Mirko   You think Kevin and the others will be nice to you? It'll be worse than before, worse than the mus–

Gio   The music room.

Mirko   Worse than the music room, yes. They'll make you lick the floor of the changing rooms which is much more –

Gio   But this time you won't let them. You won't just stand there and watch, like you did last time. (*A pause.*) I know you were there. I saw you. You were with everyone else. And you just stood there and watched. And laughed. The grosser the thing they made me do, the more you laughed. You even told them to spit on the spot they wanted me to lick. That broke my heart. Because I liked you.

Mirko   I hated myself, Gio.

Gio   Don't worry.

Mirko   I know it's all wrong!

Gio   It's okay.

Mirko   When you disappeared I felt like shit. I read every article about you online, I even came looking for you once, all by myself!

Gio   But you found me by accident, didn't you? While you were out taking pictures of woodchucks and white hares.

A pause.

Mirko   I've been a shit. We've all been shits.

Gio   It doesn't matter. Back then I liked you in a silly way, Mirko. I didn't know anything about you. Now I know you. You know me. It's different now, you'd never let anyone make me lick the floor of the music room, now.

Mirko   Gio . . .

Gio   That's right, isn't it, Mirko?

Mirko   Oh, fuck –

Gio   You're on my side now, aren't you?

Mirko   . . . Yes, of course.

Gio   That's why I want to come out, because now I know you're there. Before, I didn't even know you existed . . . but you actually . . . *exist.*

A pause.

Mirko   Okay. Listen. I'm sorry to do this but I have to take back what I said.

Gio   What?

Mirko   I thought you were strong.

Gio   I've never felt as strong as I do now.

Mirko   If you leave here, you'll fuck everything up.

Gio   But you told me it's my fault that lots of people are suffering!

Mirko   That was a test, you idiot.

Gio   Come on.

Mirko   You're doing this for fame, right?

Gio   For fame –

Mirko   You want to get interviewed, go to the TV studios, take the –

Gio   That's what you think?

Mirko   You're just like everyone else.

Gio   That I want to steal your thunder.

Mirko   You're exactly like them, Gio.

Gio   That nobody will pay you any attention if I show up?

Mirko   You're such a disappointment, Gio. You just want attention.

Gio   It's . . . *you* cut my earlobe –

Mirko   You're a child, Gio.

Gio   You're the child.

Mirko   You're only interested in going viral.

Gio   I don't care about that. I want to leave here because I want to tell everyone –

Mirko   WHAT? What do you want to tell?

Gio   Everything . . .

Mirko   What?

Gio   About Kevin and all the horrible things he and his gang do . . . they'll listen to me . . .

Mirko   That's true, you're the innocent victim, the little angel on Joseph and Mary's hut!

Gio   And I want to talk about us.

Mirko   About us?

Gio   About you and me.

Mirko   Why, for fuck's sake?

Gio   Because!

Mirko   It's our business!

Gio   It's beautiful. Kevin will have to deal with it. So will Sara. And so will my mother, and your father, and Debbie and everyone. We'll walk into school with our heads held high. Will you hold my hand?

Mirko   Jesus Christ.

Gio   You said you cared about me –

Mirko   Gio –

Gio   That you like what we –

Mirko   Fuck –

Gio   We can tell everyone, no?

Mirko   But I don't –

Gio   Are you scared?

Mirko   . . .

Gio   I'm not.

A long pause.

Mirko   Gio.

Gio   What?

Mirko   Gio . . . let's calm down for a minute, okay?

Gio   Okay.

Mirko   Calm.

Gio   Calm.

A pause.

Mirko   Gio.

Gio   Yeah?

Mirko   Do you wanna . . .

Gio   What?

Mirko   Turn off the lights.

Gio   What do you . . .

Mirko   Turn them off.

Gio   You want to –

Mirko   Turn them off.

Gio   Isn't it better if we do it outside?

Mirko   Gio.

Gio   There's lots of places we can –

Mirko   Turn the lights off.

Gio On the grass or –

Mirko Turn them off.

Gio We can go to my house, to my room, nobody will –

Mirko I want to do it. Now.

Gio I want to leave.

Mirko Okay. We will. (*A brief pause.*) But first . . .

Gio . . . yeah?

Mirko Turn off the lights.

Gio *does. The cave is plunged into darkness.*

Gio Should I undress?

Mirko Listen to me.

Gio I'll undo your –

Mirko No. Get the pillows.

Gio We don't need –

Mirko Get the pillows.

Gio Okay.

Gio *gets the pillows and holds them out.*

Here.

Mirko *lies down on the ground.*

Mirko Come here. Sit.

Gio *sits down next to him.*

Mirko Closer.

Gio *scoots closer.*

Mirko The pillow.

Gio *hands him a pillow.*

Mirko *looks at him for a few seconds.*

Mirko   I wish I could be like you, Gio. I wish I *was you*.

Gio   No. You just wish you could be *you*.

Mirko   But everything's a mess, I don't –

Gio   Yeah.

Mirko   I can't do it.

Gio   It's okay. We do what we can.

With a sudden lunge, **Mirko** *jumps on top of* **Gio**, *holding the pillow firmly down against his face.* **Gio** *struggles, his arms and legs flailing, but* **Mirko** *holds the pillow in place, pushing it down with all his strength, for a good twenty seconds.*

Until **Gio** *stops moving.*

A few more seconds pass. **Mirko**'s *breathing is ragged, he's panting.*

Then he bursts into tears. He throws himself on **Gio**'s *lifeless body, hugs it.*

He tries to stop sobbing . . . but he can't.

As the blackout slowly, slowly begins to swallow the stage, **Mirko** *stumbles to his feet and exits.*

Blackout.

Scene Eight

A few months earlier.

A TikTok reel.

A close-up of **Gio** *in his bedroom. He's clean and neat like we've never seen him.*

Looking bright and smiling.

Gio   Okay, guys, this video is dedicated to those who, like me, want to keep their hands hidden. I don't know about you, but I try to use them as little as possible. I stick them in my pockets and keep them there, as if they were in a cage. A little graveyard for my hands. A dark tunnel, where they can be at peace and not bother anyone. Sometimes I have to check that they're still alive, that they don't have insects nibbling at them. I have to move my fingers a little to keep them from atrophying. (*He shows them.*) They would like something to touch. And for something to touch them. Nobody does, nobody wants to rescue my hands from their prison, not my mum, my dad, not even the stupid cat is interested in licking them. She's only interested in her bowl of milk. But one day everything will change. Today or tomorrow, sooner or later. They say it won't, but I don't believe them. It will happen. Your hands will find mine. Life will burst through my fingers like a spurt of blood. It will blow up the cage. You will rebuild my hands. You'll be my plastic surgeon. My nails will be perfect. My hands will dance up in the attic, in the street, at the town fair. They'll interlace with yours and nobody will ever be able to tear them apart. Our hands will be so wild they'll turn into wings and together we'll be catapulted into the air. In the sky. We'll be light, agile, *aerodynamic,* every cell alive. We'll look at people from above, God, they're all so small from up here . . . We're rising higher and higher, until we can no longer tell people apart from cars or trees. The village looks like a stupid little scribble. Let's stop looking at it. Let's look up, that's where we're headed, towards that ball of light so warm and bright. It's dazzling. We have to close our eyes, but we don't need them, we don't need to see anything, we just need to know that we're together, and once we get there, when we become one with that shining sphere, we will no longer have eyes, nor ears, nor tongue, nor dick, nor ass, nor toes . . . Boom! Luminous beings in our purest state. With our whole lives ahead of us. There. That's where I'll be happy. I belong to that world. This one has honestly kinda bored me. If you have ever felt like this . . . dead and buried like my hands . . . if you too feel like you're stranded in the middle of the desert, or holding your breath underwater or just trapped without a way out . . . well, go ahead . . . comment, like and share.

Blackout.

For a complete listing of
Methuen Drama titles, visit:
www.bloomsbury.com/drama

Follow us on Twitter and keep up to date
with our news and publications
@MethuenDrama